MW01097980

High Protein

OVERNIGHT OATS

60 Quick and Easy Recipes in a Jar for a Healthy Breakfast on the Go

STELLA ROSE WILDER

INTRODUCTION

Welcome to "High Protein Overnight Oats: 60 Quick and Easy Recipes in a Jar for a Healthy Breakfast on the Go." Breakfast is often called the most important meal of the day, and with our increasingly busy lives, it's more essential than ever to have a nutritious start that also caters to our tight schedules.

This cookbook is designed to bring you the delightful fusion of convenience and health. Throughout these pages, you will discover a collection of overnight oats recipes that are not only delicious and satisfying but also packed with protein to keep you full and energized throughout the morning.

But why overnight oats? The magic of these recipes lies in their simplicity and adaptability. Prepared the night before and left to soak, the flavors meld and intensify, offering a creamy and tasty treat that's ready to grab and go come sunrise. Whether you're a fitness enthusiast seeking muscle-building proteins or someone wanting to embrace healthier morning eating habits, there's a jar in this book with your name on it.

We've focused on diverse ingredients, catering to various dietary needs, ensuring there's a mix of dairy-based, vegan, and superfood-packed options. From fruits to nuts, from traditional flavors to the more exotic, each recipe is a new adventure for your taste buds.

So, grab your mason jar, choose a recipe, and start prepping. Tomorrow's breakfast is going to be delightful!

Copyright 2023 Stella Rose Wilder

All rights reserved worldwide. No part of this book may be reproduced or transmitted in any form or by any means electronic or mechanical, including photocopying, recording or by any information storage and retrieval system without written permission from Stella Rose Wilder.

Printed in the United States of America

Stella Rose Wilder. *High Protein Overnight Oats: 60 Quick and Easy Recipes in a Jar for a Healthy Breakfast on the Go*

Disclaimer/Warning:

This book is intended for lecture and informative purposes only. This publication is designed to provide competent and reliable information regarding the subject matter covered, although inaccuracies may be present. The author or publisher are not engaged in rendering legal, medical, or professional advice. Laws vary from state to state and if legal, financial, medical, or other expert assistance is needed, the services of a professional should be sought. The information in this book is not meant to replace professional medical or nutritional advice. The author and publisher disclaim any liability that is incurred from the use or application of the contents of this book.

"Tap your snooze button with confidence knowing breakfast will be patiently waiting for you when you're ready to rise and shine."

Contents

DAIRY

BERRIES 'N CREAM OVERNIGHT OATS

Nutrition

Calories: 340, Protein: 22g, Carbohydrates: 40g, Fat: 8g, Fiber: 6g

Ingredients

1 cup oats
2 scoops strawberry protein powder
1½ cups milk
½ cup mixed berries (like strawberries, blueberries, and raspberries)
½ tsp vanilla extract

Instructions

1. In a mason jar, combine oats with strawberry protein powder.
2. Add milk, then mix in the mixed berries.
3. Add 1/2 tsp or less vanilla extract for flavor.
4. Close the jar securely and refrigerate overnight.

Prep Time
10 mins

Serving
2

TROPICAL SUNRISE OVERNIGHT OATS

Nutrition

Calories: 380, Protein: 23g, Carbohydrates: 45g, Fat: 14g, Fiber: 7g

Ingredients

1 cup oats
2 scoops vanilla protein powder
1½ cups milk
½ cup crushed pineapple
2 tbsp shredded coconut
¼ cup chopped macadamia nuts

Instructions

1. Mix oats and vanilla protein powder in the mason jar.
2. Pour in milk.
3. Add crushed pineapple and shredded coconut.
4. Garnish with chopped macadamia nuts.
5. Seal the jar and leave it in the refrigerator overnight.

Prep Time
10 mins

Serving
2

PEACHES & CREAM OVERNIGHT OATS

Nutrition

Calories: 340, Protein: 21g, Carbohydrates: 40g, Fat: 10g,
Fiber: 6g

Ingredients

1 cup oats
2 scoops vanilla protein powder
1½ cups milk
1 cup diced peaches
¼ cup almond slices

Instructions

1. Start by mixing the oats and vanilla protein powder in the jar.
2. Add the milk. Incorporate the diced peaches.
3. Top with almond slices.
4. Seal the jar and leave it in the refrigerator overnight.

**Prep Time
10 mins**

**Serving
2**

CHOCOLATE PEANUT BUTTER DELIGHT OVERNIGHT OATS

Nutrition

Calories: 360, Protein: 22g, Carbohydrates: 42g, Fat: 13g, Fiber: 6g

Ingredients

1 cup oats
2 scoops chocolate protein powder
1½ cups milk
2 tbsp peanut butter
1 banana, sliced

Instructions

1. Combine oats and chocolate protein powder in a mason jar.
2. Add in the milk, ensuring the oats are submerged.
3. Mix in peanut butter for a rich, creamy texture.
4. Top with banana slices.
5. Seal the jar and refrigerate overnight. Stir before eating.

**Prep Time
10 mins**

**Serving
2**

BANANA NUT MUFFIN OVERNIGHT OATS

Nutrition

Calories: 360, Protein: 22g, Carbohydrates: 44g, Fat: 11g, Fiber: 7g

Ingredients

1 cup oats
2 scoops vanilla protein powder
1½ cups milk
2 bananas, mashed
¼ cup walnuts, chopped
½ tsp cinnamon

Instructions

1. Combine oats and vanilla protein powder in the mason jar.
2. Pour in the milk. Add mashed bananas.
3. Sprinkle chopped walnuts and cinnamon.
4. Close the lid and refrigerate overnight. Stir well before eating.

**Prep Time
10 mins**

**Serving
2**

MAPLE PECAN OVERNIGHT OATS

Nutrition

Calories: 330, Protein: 20g, Carbohydrates: 38g, Fat: 12g,
Fiber: 5g

Ingredients

1 cup oats
2 scoops vanilla protein powder
1½ cups milk
3 tbsp pure maple syrup
½ cup chopped pecans

Instructions

1. In a mason jar, combine oats and vanilla protein powder.
2. Pour in the milk, ensuring that the oats are submerged.
3. Drizzle in the maple syrup and mix thoroughly.
4. Top with chopped pecans.
5. Close the lid securely and refrigerate overnight. Stir before eating.

**Prep Time
10 mins**

**Serving
2**

MOCHA MORNING OVERNIGHT OATS

Nutrition

Calories: 310, Protein: 21g, Carbohydrates: 34g, Fat: 8g, Fiber: 4g

Ingredients

1 cup oats
2 scoops chocolate protein powder
1 cup milk
1/2 cup cold brew coffee
1 tbsp cocoa powder

Instructions

1. In a mason jar, mix the oats and chocolate protein powder.
2. Gradually pour in the milk and cold brew coffee, mixing as you go.
3. Sprinkle in one tbsp cocoa powder and stir until well combined.
4. Close the lid tightly and refrigerate overnight.

Prep Time
10 mins

Serving
2

APPLE PIE OVERNIGHT OATS

Nutrition

Calories: 320, Protein: 19g, Carbohydrates: 40g, Fat: 8g, Fiber: 6g

Ingredients

1 cup oats
2 scoops vanilla protein powder
1½ cups milk
1 diced apple
½ tsp cinnamon
¼ tsp nutmeg

Instructions

1. In your mason jar, combine the oats and vanilla protein powder.
2. Add the milk and stir.
3. Mix in the diced apple, cinnamon, and nutmeg.
4. Seal the jar and leave it in the refrigerator overnight.

**Prep Time
10 mins**

**Serving
2**

CHERRY ALMOND OVERNIGHT OATS

Nutrition

Calories: 340, Protein: 20g, Carbohydrates: 42g, Fat: 10g, Fiber: 7g

Ingredients

1 cup oats
2 scoops vanilla protein powder
1½ cups milk
½ cup dried cherries
¼ cup chopped almonds

Instructions

1. Begin by mixing oats and vanilla protein powder in the mason jar.
2. Pour the milk over the mixture.
3. Stir in the dried cherries and chopped almonds.
4. Secure the lid and refrigerate overnight.

Prep Time
10 mins

Serving
2

MANGO LASSI TWIST OVERNIGHT OATS

Nutrition

Calories: 310, Protein: 21g, Carbohydrates: 36g, Fat: 7g, Fiber: 4g

Ingredients

1 cup oats
2 scoops vanilla protein powder
1 cup yogurt
½ cup mango pulp
¼ tsp cardamom

Instructions

1. In the mason jar, combine oats and vanilla protein powder.
2. Mix in yogurt until smooth.
3. Fold in mango pulp and sprinkle cardamom on top.
4. Close the jar tightly and refrigerate overnight. Stir before eating.

**Prep Time
10 mins**

**Serving
2**

CLASSIC ALMOND & HONEY OVERNIGHT OATS

Nutrition

Calories: 340, Protein: 18g, Carbohydrates: 45g, Fat: 14g

Ingredients

1 cup oats
1½ cups milk
2 tbsp honey
2 tbsp chia seeds
3 tbsp almond butter

Instructions

1. Combine oats, milk, honey, chia seeds, and almond butter in a mason jar.
2. Stir well to combine.
3. Seal the jar and refrigerate overnight.

Prep Time
10 mins

Serving
2

CINNAMON ROLL OVERNIGHT OATS

Nutrition

Calories: 360, Protein: 20g, Carbohydrates: 42g, Fat: 10g

Ingredients

1 cup oats
1½ cups milk
¾ cup cottage cheese
1 tsp cinnamon
¼ cup raisins
2 tbsp hemp seeds

Instructions

1. Mix in oats, milk, and cottage cheese in a mason jar.
2. Add in cinnamon, raisins, and hemp seeds.
3. Drizzle with honey.
4. Seal the jar and refrigerate overnight.

**Prep Time
10 mins**

**Serving
2**

RASPBERRY CHEESECAKE OVERNIGHT OATS

Nutrition

Calories: 370, Protein: 22g, Carbohydrates: 40g, Fat: 16g

Ingredients

1 cup oats
1 cup Greek yogurt
½ cup fresh raspberries
3 tbsp almond butter
2 tbsp chia seeds

Instructions

1. Start by placing oats and Greek yogurt in the mason jar.
2. Add fresh raspberries and almond butter.
3. Sprinkle with chia seeds.
4. Close the jar securely and refrigerate overnight.

**Prep Time
10 mins**

**Serving
2**

BLUEBERRY PANCAKE OVERNIGHT OATS

Nutrition

Calories: 340, Protein: 18g, Carbohydrates: 42g, Fat: 14g

Ingredients

1 cup oats
1½ cups milk
½ cup fresh blueberries
2 tbsp maple syrup
¼ cup chopped walnuts
2 tbsp flax seeds

Instructions

1. Combine oats and milk in the mason jar.
2. Mix in fresh blueberries, flax seeds, and maple syrup.
3. Top with chopped walnuts.
4. Seal the jar and leave it in the refrigerator overnight.

Prep Time
10 mins

Serving
2

STRAWBERRIES 'N CREAM OVERNIGHT OATS

Nutrition

Calories: 320, Protein: 20g, Carbohydrates: 40g, Fat: 12g

Ingredients

1 cup oats
1 cup Greek yogurt
½ cup fresh strawberries, sliced
2 tbsp chia seeds
2 tbsp hemp seeds
½ tsp vanilla extract

Instructions

1. In a mason jar, mix oats with Greek yogurt.
2. Incorporate the sliced strawberries.
3. Add chia, hemp, and a hint of vanilla for flavor.
4. Close the jar securely and refrigerate overnight.

Prep Time
10 mins

Serving
2

PISTACHIO ROSE OVERNIGHT OATS

Nutrition

Calories: 286, Protein: 16g, Carbohydrates: 33g, Fat: 12g

Ingredients

1 cup oats
1½ cups milk
½ cup crushed pistachios
1 tsp rose water
2 tbsp honey
2 tbsp chia seeds

Instructions

1. Combine oats and milk in a mason jar.
2. Mix in crushed pistachios with rose water and honey.
3. Stir in chia seeds for added protein.
4. Seal and refrigerate overnight.

**Prep Time
10 mins**

**Serving
2**

PINEAPPLE COCONUT CRUSH OVERNIGHT OATS

Nutrition

Calories: 276, Protein: 18g, Carbohydrates: 28g, Fat: 10g

Ingredients

1 cup oats
1 cup Greek yogurt
½ cup crushed pineapple
¼ cup shredded coconut
2 tbsp honey
2 tbsp chia seeds

Instructions

1. Mix oats with Greek yogurt in a mason jar.
2. Add in crushed pineapple, shredded coconut, and honey.
3. Stir in chia seeds for an extra protein boost.
4. Seal and refrigerate overnight.

**Prep Time
10 mins**

**Serving
2**

PEANUT BUTTER BANANA OVERNIGHT OATS

Nutrition

Calories: 350, Protein: 17g, Carbohydrates: 48g, Fat: 10g

Ingredients

1 cup oats
1½ cups milk
4 tbsp peanut butter powder
1 banana, sliced
2 tbsp honey
2 tbsp chia seeds

Instructions

1. In a mason jar, combine oats and milk.
2. Mix in peanut butter powder, sliced banana, and honey.
3. Incorporate chia seeds for added protein.
4. Seal and refrigerate overnight.

**Prep Time
10 mins**

**Serving
2**

MIXED BERRY PARFAIT OVERNIGHT OATS

Nutrition

Calories: 330, Protein: 19g, Carbohydrates: 43g, Fat: 11g

Ingredients

1 cup oats
1 cup Greek yogurt
½ cup mixed berries (strawberries, blueberries, raspberries)
¼ cup almond slices
2 tbsp chia seeds

Instructions

1. Mix oats and Greek yogurt in a mason jar.
2. Add in the mixed berries.
3. Sprinkle with almond slices and chia seeds.
4. Seal and refrigerate overnight.

Prep Time
10 mins

Serving
2

CHOCOLATE HAZELNUT BLISS OVERNIGHT OATS

Nutrition

Calories: 360, Protein: 17g, Carbohydrates: 45g, Fat: 14g

Ingredients

1 cup oats
1½ cups milk
3 tbsp cocoa powder
3 tbsp hazelnut butter
2 tbsp chia seeds

Instructions

1. In a mason jar, mix oats with milk.
2. Add cocoa powder and hazelnut butter.
3. Stir in chia seeds to up the protein content.
4. Seal and refrigerate overnight.

**Prep Time
10 mins**

**Serving
2**

CARAMEL MACCHIATO OVERNIGHT OATS

Nutrition

Calories: 360, Protein: 21g, Carbohydrates: 44g, Fat: 9g, Fiber: 5g

Ingredients

1 cup oats
2 scoops protein powder
1½ cups espresso-infused milk
1 tbsp caramel extract

Instructions

1. In a mason jar, combine the oats and protein powder. Pour in the espresso-infused milk, ensuring that the oats are completely covered.
2. Mix in the caramel extract, blending it well with the mixture. Seal the jar and place it in the refrigerator overnight. Give it a good stir before enjoying it.

**Prep Time
10 mins**

**Serving
2**

29

CREAMY CASHEW CINNAMON SWIRL OVERNIGHT OATS

Nutrition

Calories: 370, Protein: 15g, Carbohydrates: 48g, Fat: 15g, Fiber: 7g

Ingredients

1 cup oats
1½ cups milk
1/2 cup chopped cashews
2 tsp cinnamon
1 tbsp flaxseeds

Instructions

1. Begin by placing the oats into a mason jar.
2. Pour in the milk, ensuring all oats are well-submerged.
3. Add the chopped cashews to the mix, followed by the cinnamon for that warm, spicy flavor.
4. Lastly, sprinkle in the flaxseeds, giving the mixture a final stir.
5. Seal the jar and refrigerate overnight. Stir thoroughly before eating.

**Prep Time
10 mins**

**Serving
2**

PASSION FRUIT PROTEIN FUSION OVERNIGHT OATS

Nutrition

Calories: 340, Protein: 20g, Carbohydrates: 40g, Fat: 11g, Fiber: 6g

Ingredients

1 cup oats
2 scoops protein powder
1½ cups yogurt
Pulp of 2 passion fruits
1/4 cup almond slivers

Instructions

1. In a mason jar, combine oats and protein powder.
2. Mix in the yogurt until the mixture is smooth.
3. Fold in the passion fruit pulp and almond slivers, ensuring an even distribution.
4. Seal the jar and refrigerate overnight. Stir before enjoying.

**Prep Time
10 mins**

**Serving
2**

GINGER PEACH PICK-ME-UP OVERNIGHT OATS

Nutrition

Calories: 360, Protein: 22g, Carbohydrates: 42g, Fat: 13g, Fiber: 6g

Ingredients

1 cup oats
1½ cups milk
1 peach, diced
1 tsp ginger powder
1 tbsp honey
2 tbsp hemp seeds

Instructions

1. Place oats into a mason jar.
2. Add the milk, ensuring the oats are submerged.
3. Incorporate the diced peaches and ginger powder into the mixture.
4. Drizzle in honey for sweetness and sprinkle hemp seeds for an added crunch.
5. Seal the jar and refrigerate overnight. Stir well before consuming.

**Prep Time
10 mins**

**Serving
2**

CHERRY CHOCOLATE CHUNK OVERNIGHT OATS

Nutrition

Calories: 316, Protein: 18g, Carbohydrates: 34g, Fat: 13g, Fiber: 5g

Ingredients

1 cup oats
2 scoops chocolate protein powder
1½ cups milk
1/2 cup cherries, pitted and halved
1/4 cup coconut flakes
1 tbsp maple syrup

Instructions

1. In a mason jar, mix oats and chocolate protein powder.
2. Pour in the milk with maple syrup and ensuring the oats are fully covered.
3. Add the cherries and sprinkle with coconut flakes.
4. Seal the jar and place it in the refrigerator overnight. Stir thoroughly before savoring.

**Prep Time
10 mins**

**Serving
2**

VEGAN

VEGAN CHOCOLATE COCONUT OVERNIGHT OATS

Nutrition

Calories: 330, Protein: 24g, Carbohydrates: 40g, Fat: 9g

Ingredients

1 cup oats
1½ cups almond milk
2 scoops chocolate plant-based protein powder
4 tbsp shredded coconut
2 tbsp cocoa nibs

Instructions

1. In a mason jar, combine oats with almond milk.
2. Stir in chocolate plant-based protein powder.
3. Mix in shredded coconut and cocoa nibs.
4. Seal and refrigerate overnight.

**Prep Time
10 mins**

**Serving
2**

GREEN MATCHA DELIGHT OVERNIGHT OATS

Nutrition

Calories: 350, Protein: 25g, Carbohydrates: 44g, Fat: 12g

Ingredients

1 cup oats
1½ cups coconut milk
2 scoops vanilla plant-based protein powder
1 tbsp matcha powder
3 tbsp chia seeds

Instructions

1. In a mason jar, mix oats with coconut milk.
2. Blend in vanilla plant-based protein powder and matcha powder.
3. Fold in chia seeds for added protein.
4. Seal and refrigerate overnight.

**Prep Time
10 mins**

**Serving
2**

PUMPKIN PIE OVERNIGHT OATS

Nutrition

Calories: 310, Protein: 23g, Carbohydrates: 40g, Fat: 8g

Ingredients

1 cup oats
1½ cups almond milk
2 scoops vanilla plant-based protein
powder
½ cup pumpkin puree
1 tsp pumpkin spice

Instructions

1. In a mason jar, combine oats with almond milk.
2. Mix in vanilla plant-based protein powder and pumpkin puree.
3. Season with pumpkin spice.
4. Seal and put it aside in the refrigerator overnight.

**Prep Time
10 mins**

**Serving
2**

GOLDEN TURMERIC & CHIA OVERNIGHT OATS

Nutrition

Calories: 360, Protein: 26g, Carbohydrates: 46g, Fat: 13g

Ingredients

1 cup oats
1½ cups coconut milk
2 scoops vanilla plant-based protein powder
3 tbsp chia seeds
1 tsp turmeric

Instructions

1. In a mason jar, mix oats with coconut milk.
2. Stir in vanilla plant-based protein powder.
3. Add chia seeds and turmeric.
4. Seal and refrigerate overnight.

**Prep Time
10 mins**

**Serving
2**

TROPICAL VEGAN DREAM OVERNIGHT OATS

Nutrition

Calories: 320, Protein: 23g, Carbohydrates: 39g, Fat: 7g

Ingredients

1 cup oats
1½ cups almond milk
2 scoops vanilla plant-based protein powder
½ cup diced mango
2 tbsp passionfruit pulp

Instructions

1. In a mason jar, blend oats with almond milk.
2. Incorporate vanilla plant-based protein powder.
3. Mix in diced mango and passionfruit pulp.
4. Seal and put it aside in the refrigerator overnight.

**Prep Time
10 mins**

**Serving
2**

COCOA BANANA OVERNIGHT OATS

Nutrition

Calories: 340, Protein: 28g, Carbohydrates: 48g, Fat: 10g

Ingredients

1 cup oats
1½ cups oat milk
2 scoops chocolate plant-based protein powder
1 sliced banana
2 tbsp almond butter

Instructions

1. In a mason jar, mix oats with oat milk.
2. Add the chocolate protein powder and stir until blended.
3. Mix in sliced bananas.
4. Top with almond butter.
5. Seal the jar and refrigerate overnight.

**Prep Time
10 mins**

**Serving
2**

Vegan

BERRY PROTEIN POWER OVERNIGHT OATS

Nutrition

Calories: 320, Protein: 27g, Carbohydrates: 44g, Fat: 8g

Ingredients

1 cup oats
1½ cups almond milk
2 scoops of berry plant-based protein
powder
1 cup mixed berries
1 tbsp flaxseeds

Instructions

1. Combine oats and almond milk in a mason jar.
2. Stir in the berry protein powder.
3. Add mixed berries and flaxseeds.
4. Seal the jar and put it aside in the refrigerator overnight.

**Prep Time
10 mins**

**Serving
2**

CHAI SPICED OVERNIGHT OATS

Nutrition

Calories: 360, Protein: 26g, Carbohydrates: 40g, Fat: 14g

Ingredients

1 cup oats
1½ cups coconut milk
2 scoops vanilla plant-based protein powder
1 tsp chai spices

Instructions

1. Mix oats with coconut milk in a mason jar.
2. Blend in the vanilla protein powder.
3. Add chai spices and mix well.
4. Seal the jar and refrigerate overnight.

**Prep Time
10 mins**

**Serving
2**

MAPLE WALNUT VEGAN CRUNCH OVERNIGHT OATS

Nutrition

Calories: 330, Protein: 25g, Carbohydrates: 42g, Fat: 12g

Ingredients

1 cup oats
1½ cups almond milk
2 scoops of maple plant-based protein powder
¼ cup chopped walnuts

Instructions

1. In a mason jar, mix oats with almond milk.
2. Incorporate maple protein powder.
3. Top with chopped walnuts.
4. Seal the jar and let it chill overnight.

Prep Time
10 mins

Serving
2

PINA COLADA OVERNIGHT OATS

Nutrition

Calories: 350, Protein: 27g, Carbohydrates: 46g, Fat: 11g

Ingredients

1 cup oats
1½ cups coconut milk
2 scoops vanilla plant-based protein powder
½ cup crushed pineapple
2 tbsp shredded coconut

Instructions

1. Combine oats and coconut milk in a mason jar.
2. Blend in the vanilla protein powder.
3. Add crushed pineapple and shredded coconut.
4. Seal the jar and refrigerate overnight.

**Prep Time
10 mins**

**Serving
2**

VANILLA ALMOND JOY OVERNIGHT OATS

Nutrition

Calories: 320, Protein: 12g, Carbohydrates: 42g, Fat: 14g

Ingredients

1 cup oats
1½ cups almond milk
3 tbsp almond butter
2 tbsp chia seeds
1 tsp vanilla extract

Instructions

1. In a mason jar, mix oats with almond milk.
2. Stir in almond butter until smooth.
3. Add chia seeds and vanilla extract.
4. Seal the jar and refrigerate overnight.

**Prep Time
10 mins**

**Serving
2**

SWEET FIG & PECAN OVERNIGHT OATS

Nutrition

Calories: 340, Protein: 9g, Carbohydrates: 52g, Fat: 13g

Ingredients

1 cup oats
1½ cups almond milk
¼ cup chopped dried figs
3 tbsp crushed pecans
2 tbsp maple syrup

Instructions

1. Combine oats and almond milk in a mason jar.
2. Mix in the dried figs and crushed pecans.
3. Drizzle with maple syrup.
4. Seal the jar and refrigerate overnight.

Prep Time
10 mins

Serving
2

TROPICAL FLAX DELIGHT OVERNIGHT OATS

Nutrition

Calories: 330, Protein: 8g, Carbohydrates: 45g, Fat: 15g

Ingredients

1 cup oats
1½ cups coconut milk
½ cup diced mango
½ cup kiwi slices
2 tbsp flaxseeds

Instructions

1. Mix oats with coconut milk in a mason jar.
2. Add diced mango and kiwi slices.
3. Stir in flaxseeds.
4. Seal the jar and refrigerate overnight.

Prep Time
10 mins

Serving
2

47

BLUEBERRY HEMP OVERNIGHT OATS

Nutrition

Calories: 310, Protein: 11g, Carbohydrates: 47g, Fat: 10g

Ingredients

1 cup oats
1½ cups oat milk
1 cup fresh blueberries
2 tbsp hemp seeds
1 tbsp maple syrup

Instructions

1. Combine oats and oat milk in a mason jar.
2. Mix in fresh blueberries and hemp seeds.
3. Drizzle with a touch of maple syrup.
4. Seal and refrigerate overnight.

**Prep Time
10 mins**

**Serving
2**

CRANBERRY WALNUT CRUNCH OVERNIGHT OATS

Nutrition

Calories: 320, Protein: 9g, Carbohydrates: 49g, Fat: 12g

Ingredients

1 cup oats
1½ cups almond milk
¼ cup dried cranberries
3 tbsp chopped walnuts
1 tbsp agave nectar

Instructions

1. Mix oats with almond milk in a mason jar.
2. Add dried cranberries and chopped walnuts.
3. Drizzle with agave nectar.
4. Seal the jar and put it aside in the refrigerator overnight.

**Prep Time
10 mins**

**Serving
2**

ZESTY ORANGE & COCOA OVERNIGHT OATS

Nutrition

Calories: 310, Protein: 10g, Carbohydrates: 46g, Fat: 11g

Ingredients

1 cup oats
1½ cups oat milk
Zest of 1 orange
3 tbsp cocoa nibs
2 tbsp chia seeds

Instructions

1. In a mason jar, mix oats with oat milk.
2. Stir in orange zest and cocoa nibs.
3. Add chia seeds for added protein and texture.
4. Seal the jar and refrigerate overnight.

**Prep Time
10 mins**

**Serving
2**

Vegan

MOCHA CHIA WAKE-UP OVERNIGHT OATS

Nutrition

Calories: 320, Protein: 11g, Carbohydrates: 47g, Fat: 10g

Ingredients

1 cup oats
1 cup almond milk
1/2 cup cold brew coffee
2 tbsp cocoa powder
2 tbsp chia seeds

Instructions

1. Combine oats, almond milk and cold brew coffee in a mason jar.
2. Mix in the cocoa powder.
3. Add chia seeds for a protein boost.
4. Seal the jar and refrigerate overnight.

**Prep Time
10 mins**

**Serving
2**

SESAME DATE DELIGHT OVERNIGHT OATS

Nutrition

Calories: 330, Protein: 9g, Carbohydrates: 55g, Fat: 9g

Ingredients

1 cup oats
1½ cups almond milk
¼ cup chopped dates
2 tbsp sesame seeds
1 tbsp agave nectar

Instructions

1. Mix oats with almond milk in a mason jar.
2. Add chopped dates and sesame seeds.
3. Drizzle with agave nectar.
4. Seal the jar and refrigerate overnight.

**Prep Time
10 mins**

**Serving
2**

Vegan

GOLDEN RAISIN SUNFLOWER OVERNIGHT OATS

Nutrition

Calories: 340, Protein: 11g, Carbohydrates: 53g, Fat: 10g

Ingredients

1 cup oats
1½ cups oat milk
¼ cup golden raisins
3 tbsp sunflower seeds
1 tbsp maple syrup

Instructions

1. Combine oats and oat milk in a mason jar.
2. Mix in golden raisins and sunflower seeds.
3. Drizzle with maple syrup.
4. Seal and refrigerate overnight.

**Prep Time
10 mins**

**Serving
2**

Vegan

BLACKBERRY BASIL BLISS OVERNIGHT OATS

Nutrition

Calories: 310, Protein: 11g, Carbohydrates: 47g, Fat: 9g

Ingredients

1 cup oats
1½ cups almond milk
1 cup fresh blackberries
2 tbsp chia seeds
5-6 fresh basil leaves, finely chopped

Instructions

1. Mix oats with almond milk in a mason jar.
2. Add fresh blackberries and chia seeds.
3. Stir in finely chopped basil for a refreshing twist.
4. Seal the jar and put it aside in the refrigerator overnight.

**Prep Time
10 mins**

**Serving
2**

Vegan

RASPBERRY ROSE RENEWAL OVERNIGHT OATS

Nutrition

Calories: 320, Protein: 12g, Carbohydrates: 44g, Fat: 10g, Fiber: 8g

Ingredients

1 cup oats
1½ cups soy milk
1/2 cup raspberries
1 tsp rose extract
2 tbsp flaxseeds

Instructions

1. In a mason jar, combine oats and soy milk.
2. Add raspberries and mix gently.
3. Stir in rose extract for a delicate floral hint.
4. Sprinkle with flaxseeds for added nutrition.
5. Seal the jar and refrigerate overnight. Stir before enjoying.

**Prep Time
10 mins**

**Serving
2**

Vegan

SPICED APPLE ALMOND CRUMBLE OVERNIGHT OATS

Nutrition

Calories: 380, Protein: 18g, Carbohydrates: 50g, Fat: 14g, Fiber: 5g

Ingredients

1 cup oats
1½ cups cashew milk
1/2 cup stewed apples
1 tsp cinnamon
1/4 tsp nutmeg
1/4 cup crushed almonds

Instructions

1. In a mason jar, mix oats with cashew milk.
2. Incorporate the stewed apples into the mixture.
3. Season with cinnamon and nutmeg for a spiced touch.
4. Top with crushed almonds for crunch.
5. Seal the jar and refrigerate overnight. Mix well before serving.

**Prep Time
10 mins**

**Serving
2**

Vegan

POMEGRANATE PISTACHIO PERFEC-TION OVERNIGHT OATS

Nutrition

Calories: 330, Protein: 11g, Carbohydrates: 48g, Fat: 11g, Fiber: 7g

Ingredients

1 cup oats
1½ cups almond milk
1/2 cup pomegranate arils
1/4 cup pistachios
2 tbsp maple syrup or agave

Instructions

1. Place oats in a mason jar and pour in almond milk.
2. Add pomegranate arils and pistachios, stirring gently.
3. Drizzle with maple syrup or agave.
4. Seal and refrigerate overnight. Stir well before digging in.

**Prep Time
10 mins**

**Serving
2**

Vegan

CRAN-APPLE CINNAMON CRUNCH OVERNIGHT OATS

Nutrition

Calories: 370, Protein: 9g, Carbohydrates: 42g, Fat: 20g, Fiber: 7g

Ingredients

1 cup oats
1½ cups coconut milk
1/4 cup cranberries
1/2 apple, diced
1 tsp cinnamon
1/4 cup walnuts

Instructions

1. Mix oats and coconut milk in a mason jar.
2. Add cranberries and diced apples to the mixture.
3. Sprinkle cinnamon for a warming spice.
4. Top with walnuts for added texture.
5. Seal the jar and refrigerate overnight. Mix well before eating.

**Prep Time
10 mins**

**Serving
2**

PEAR & GRANOLA OVERNIGHT OATS

Nutrition

Calories: 350, Protein: 10g, Carbohydrates: 52g, Fat: 12g, Fiber: 9g

Ingredients

1 cup oats
1½ cups rice or almond milk
1 pear, diced
1/4 cup granola
2 tbsp chia seeds

Instructions

1. In a mason jar, combine oats and your choice of milk.
2. Incorporate the diced pear pieces.
3. Add granola for a delightful crunch.
4. Mix in chia seeds for a protein boost.
5. Seal and refrigerate overnight. Stir thoroughly before relishing.

**Prep Time
10 mins**

**Serving
2**

SUPERFOOD

GOJI BERRY BOOST OVERNIGHT OATS

Nutrition

Calories: 320, Protein: 10g, Carbohydrates: 50g, Fat: 9g

Ingredients

1 cup oats
1½ cups milk
¼ cup goji berries
2 tbsp chia seeds
1 tbsp honey

Instructions

1. Start by pouring oats into a mason jar.
2. Add milk, ensuring the oats are well submerged.
3. Incorporate the goji berries, which soften overnight and provide a delightful chewy texture.
4. Mix in chia seeds to give an added protein and fiber boost.
5. Finish off by drizzling in the honey for a touch of natural sweetness.
6. Seal the jar tightly and refrigerate overnight, allowing all the ingredients to meld together.

**Prep Time
10 mins**

**Serving
2**

SPIRULINA SEA BREEZE OVERNIGHT OATS

Nutrition

Calories: 360, Protein: 8g, Carbohydrates: 45g, Fat: 16g

Ingredients

1 cup oats
1½ cups coconut milk
1 tsp spirulina powder
½ cup pineapple chunks
2 tbsp shredded coconut

Instructions

1. In a mason jar, combine oats with creamy coconut milk.
2. Sprinkle in spirulina powder, a superfood known for its rich nutrients and vibrant color.
3. Add in juicy pineapple chunks to bring a tropical twist to the mix.
4. Mix in the shredded coconut for an extra burst of flavor and texture.
5. Seal the jar, and let the oats soak and flavors intensify overnight in the refrigerator.

Prep Time
10 mins

Serving
2

CACAO & MACA ENERGIZER OVERNIGHT OATS

Nutrition

Calories: 340, Protein: 9g, Carbohydrates: 47g, Fat: 12g

Ingredients

1 cup oats
1½ cups almond milk
2 tbsp cacao powder
1 tsp maca powder
1 tbsp agave nectar

Instructions

1. Pour oats into a mason jar and add almond milk.
2. Mix in cacao powder for a rich chocolatey flavor.
3. Incorporate maca powder, a superfood known to enhance energy and stamina.
4. Sweeten the mix with agave nectar, adjusting according to your preference.
5. After sealing the jar, refrigerate overnight, allowing the flavors to merge and the oats to soften.

Prep Time
10 mins

Serving
2

BLUEBERRY ACAI POWERHOUSE OVERNIGHT OATS

Nutrition

Calories: 310, Protein: 11g, Carbohydrates: 44g, Fat: 8g

Ingredients

1 cup oats
1 cup yogurt
½ cup fresh blueberries
1 tsp acai powder
1 tbsp honey

Instructions

1. Combine oats and yogurt in a mason jar.
2. Gently fold in fresh blueberries.
3. Mix in the acai powder for an antioxidant boost.
4. Drizzle honey to enhance sweetness.
5. Tightly seal the jar (it should be air-sealed) and place it in the refrigerator overnight, ensuring the flavors meld together.

Prep Time
10 mins

Serving
2

MORINGA MINT FRESHNESS OVERNIGHT OATS

Nutrition

Calories: 330, Protein: 7g, Carbohydrates: 42g, Fat: 15g

Ingredients

1 cup oats
1½ cups coconut milk
1 tsp moringa powder
1 cup fresh mint leaves, finely chopped
1 tbsp agave nectar

Instructions

1. Begin by mixing oats with coconut milk in a mason jar.
2. Add moringa powder, a superfood known for its health benefits.
3. Incorporate the finely chopped mint leaves, offering a refreshing touch.
4. Sweeten with agave nectar.
5. Seal the jar and refrigerate overnight, allowing the diverse ingredients to blend and create a delightful morning treat.

**Prep Time
10 mins**

**Serving
2**

GOLDENBERRY & QUINOA CRUNCH OVERNIGHT OATS

Nutrition

Calories: 320, Protein: 10g, Carbohydrates: 55g, Fat: 8g

Ingredients

1 cup oats
1½ cups milk
½ cup dried goldenberries
½ cup cooked quinoa
3 tbsp maple syrup

Instructions

1. In a mason jar, combine oats and milk. Mix until oats are well-soaked.
2. Fold in the dried goldenberries and cooked quinoa, ensuring even distribution.
3. Drizzle in maple syrup, mixing well to incorporate the sweet flavor throughout.
4. Seal the jar and let it rest in the refrigerator overnight.
5. Serve chilled in the morning. Add ¼ cup more milk or some extra goldenberries on top if desired.

**Prep Time
10 mins**

**Serving
2**

ASHWAGANDHA ALMOND DREAM OVERNIGHT OATS

Nutrition

Calories: 340, Protein: 9g, Carbohydrates: 47g, Fat: 12g

Ingredients

1 cup oats
1½ cups almond milk
1 tsp ashwagandha powder
3 tbsp almond butter
3 tbsp agave nectar

Instructions

1. Begin by mixing the oats with almond milk in a mason jar.
2. Add the ashwagandha powder to the jar and mix thoroughly.
3. Incorporate almond butter for a creamy texture and rich flavor.
4. Sweeten the mixture with agave nectar, stirring well to combine.
5. Close the jar and leave it in the fridge overnight.
6. In the morning, give it a good stir and enjoy.

Prep Time
10 mins

Serving
2

CHLORELLA CHERRY CHILLER OVERNIGHT OATS

Nutrition

Calories: 360, Protein: 8g, Carbohydrates: 45g, Fat: 15g

Ingredients

1 cup oats
1½ cups coconut milk
1 tsp chlorella powder
½ cup fresh cherries, pitted and halved
2 tbsp chia seeds

Instructions

1. Mix oats with coconut milk in a mason jar until well combined.
2. Sprinkle in the chlorella powder, stirring to ensure no clumps.
3. Add in the fresh cherries and chia seeds.
4. Seal the jar and refrigerate overnight.
5. Enjoy a refreshing and healthy breakfast the next day.

**Prep Time
10 mins**

**Serving
2**

FLAX & BAOBAB SUNRISE OVERNIGHT OATS

Nutrition

Calories: 310, Protein: 9g, Carbohydrates: 48g, Fat: 10g

Ingredients

1 cup oats
1½ cups oat milk
3 tbsp flaxseeds
1 tsp baobab powder
½ cup sliced strawberries

Instructions

1. In your mason jar, blend the oats with oat milk.
2. Add the flaxseeds and baobab powder, mixing thoroughly.
3. Top with fresh strawberry slices, pushing some down into the mixture.
4. Seal and let the jar sit in the fridge overnight.
5. Stir before eating, and add more strawberries if desired.

**Prep Time
10 mins**

**Serving
2**

CAMU CAMU CITRUS PUNCH OVERNIGHT OATS

Nutrition

Calories: 320, Protein: 7g, Carbohydrates: 50g, Fat: 9g

Ingredients

1 cup oats
1½ cups almond milk
1 tsp camu camu powder
½ cup orange slices
3 tbsp agave nectar

Instructions

1. Start by soaking the oats in almond milk in a mason jar.
2. Incorporate the camu camu powder, stirring well.
3. Add in fresh orange slices for a citrusy punch.
4. Sweeten the preparation with agave nectar and mix well.
5. Seal the jar and place it in the refrigerator overnight.
6. Serve chilled, and enjoy the zesty flavors.

**Prep Time
10 mins**

**Serving
2**

CONCLUSION

As we reach the end of this culinary journey, I hope you've found inspiration in each jar and have come to appreciate the beauty of combining nutrition with convenience. These overnight oats recipes are more than just breakfast; they represent a commitment to healthier mornings, to savoring flavors, and to nourishing ourselves even on the busiest days. Remember, each jar you prepare is a step toward wellness and a delicious start to your day. Here's to many mornings filled with protein-packed goodness and the simple joys found in a jar of overnight oats. Cheers!

Made in the USA
Columbia, SC
17 November 2024

46777228R00041